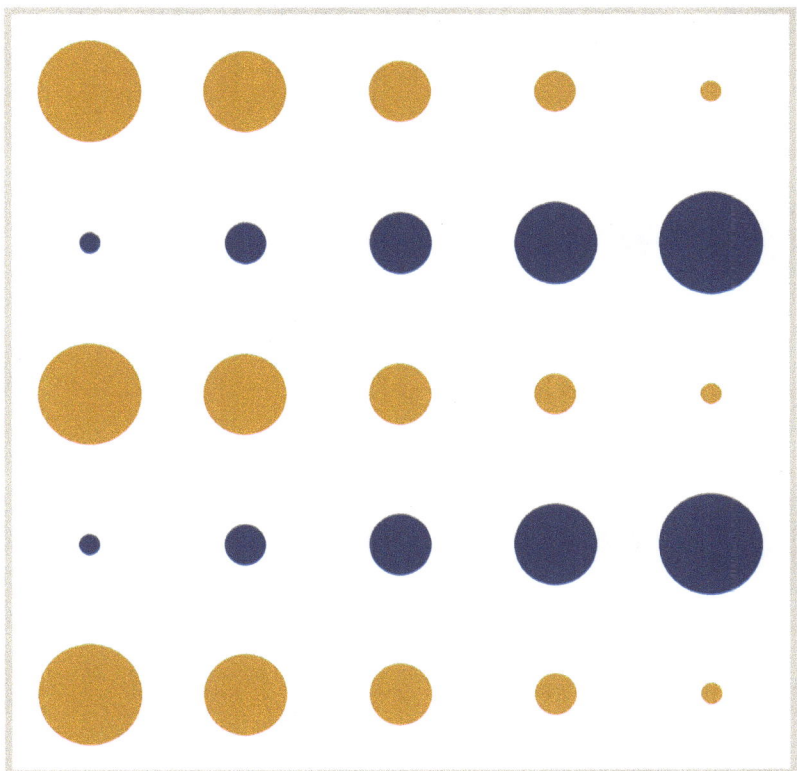

Dotty Spotty

Crochet Blankets by Shelley Husband

CLASSIC CIRCLE-TO-SQUARE GRANNY SQUARE FUN

Copyright © 2022 by Shelley Husband
All rights reserved. No part of this publication may be reproduced or transmitted by any means, electronic, photocopying or otherwise without prior written permission of the author.

ISBN-13: 978-0-6451573-8-3

Charts by Amy Gunderson
Email: kinglouiespizza@gmail.com
Ravelry ID: AmyGunderson

Graphic Design by Michelle Lorimer
Email: hello@michellelorimer.com

Blanket Photography by Jo O'Keefe
Email: jookeefe@hotmail.com
Instagram: missfarmerjojo

Other Photography by Shelley Husband

Technical Editing by SiewBee Pond
Email: essbee1995@yahoo.com

First edition 2022

Published by Shelley Husband

PO Box 11
Narrawong VIC 3285
Australia

shelleyhusbandcrochet.com

080623

CONTENTS

4 Welcome
- *What is the Dotty Spotty Crochet Blanket Pattern?*

5 You will need
- *The Original Dotty Spotty Baby Blanket*
- *The Random Dotty Spotty Baby Blanket*
- *The Dotty Spotty Big Kid Blanket*

10 General help

21 The patterns
- *1 Round Dot*
- *2 Round Dot*
- *3 Round Dot*
- *4 Round Dot*
- *5 Round Dot*

32 Blanket instructions
- *The Original Dotty Spotty Baby Blanket*
- *The Random Dotty Spotty Baby Blanket*
- *The Dotty Spotty Big Kid Blanket*

40 Make it your own
- *Plan your layout*
- *Yarn calculations*
- *Yarn needs worksheet*
- *Colouring page*

46 Glossary

48 Left-handed charts

51 Helpful links

52 Thank you

53 About the author

54 More books by Shelley Husband

WELCOME

What is the Dotty Spotty Crochet Blanket Pattern?

I designed the original Dotty Spotty Baby Blanket pattern back in 2015 for a then work colleague's new bub. It was originally released as a very basic PDF pattern. Since then, my skills in pattern writing and publishing have greatly improved. And so, here you find the new and improved Dotty Spotty Blanket pattern.

I want you to take the information here and create your own Dotty Spotty wonders. There are so many fun possibilities and, while I give you three examples of different ways you can use the patterns to make blankets, I have also provided all the information and support you need to design and create your own Dotty Spotty blanket joy.

YOU WILL NEED

Here you'll find the yarn and hook needs for the three Dotty Spotty samples I made.

The Original Dotty Spotty Baby Blanket

This is a reproduction as close as I could make to the 2015 yellow and green version. The original green colour I used has now been discontinued so I used the closest match, which is a bit brighter.

**Bendigo Woollen Mills Cotton
8 ply/DK/light worsted**

485 metres/530 yards per 200 gram ball

Metres/yards per gram: 2.43/2.66

Hook: 4.5 mm

Blanket size: 90 cm/35 in

Daffodil (yellow): 55 grams/134 metres/147 yards of 1 ball used

Pine Lime (green): 60 grams/145 metres/159 yards of 1 ball used

Parchment (neutral): 330 grams/800 metres/875 yards of 2 balls used

The Random Dotty Spotty Baby Blanket

For this version, I used mostly white and sprinkled through some blue dots in a random-ish fashion.

Bendigo Woollen Mills Cotton
10 ply/aran/worsted

360 metres/393 yards per 200 gram ball

Metres/yards per gram: 1.8/1.97

Hook: 5.5 mm

Blanket size: 102 cm/40 in

French Navy (dark blue): 30 grams/54 metres/59 yards of 1 ball used

Ice (pale blue): 30 grams/54 metres/59 yards of 1 ball used

Snow (white): 600 grams/1,080 metres/1,182 yards of 3 balls used

The Dotty Spotty Big Kid Blanket

Babies grow up to be big kids very quickly. Which is why I made this larger version for those little babes growing up and moving into big kid beds.

Bendigo Woollen Mills Cotton
10 ply/aran/worsted

360 metres/393 yards per 200 gram ball

Metres/yards per gram: 1.8/1.97

Hook: 5.5 mm

Blanket size: 142 x 180 cm/56 x 71 in

French Navy (dark blue): 280 grams/505 metres/553 yards of 2 balls used

Golden Glow (mustard): 190 grams/342 metres/375 yards of 1 ball used

Parchment (natural): 1,300 grams/2,340 metres/2,600 yards of 7 balls used

GENERAL HELP

This section will give you the help you might need to make the Dotty Spotty pattern. Lots of helpful hints and tips to make your dots and squares sing. You will see how to access the videos on the Helpful links section on page 47.

How to read the patterns and charts

Reading the written patterns

The abbreviations of all the stitches and techniques used in the written patterns and charts are explained in full in the Glossary on page 46.

Here's an excerpt from the 3 Round Dot pattern on page 26:

R3: ch3 (stch), tr in same st as ss, *tr in next st**, 2tr in next st*, rep from * to * 10x and * to ** 1x, join with ss to 3rd ch of stch. Fasten off. {36 sts}

After the beginning of round instructions, the first single asterisk indicates the start of a repeat and the second single asterisk indicates the end of a full repeat. The double asterisks indicate the end of a partial repeat. Ignore the asterisks and follow the instructions until you get to "rep". That is your cue to go back to the first single asterisk and redo the pattern repeat as many times in full and partially as instructed. After the repeats, I tell you how to finish off the round.

Brackets

(xxxx) are stitches and/or chain spaces that are all worked in the one stitch or space.

{xxxx} contain the stitch count for each round. When the shape is a circle, then it describes how many stitches in total make up that round. When the shape is square, it states how many stitches are along each side between the corners and describes the corners.

Reading the charts

The charts are visual representations of the written patterns. Every stitch of the pattern is shown where it is worked.

The Glossary on page 46 shows what stitch each symbol represents.

Work to the left from the small red round numbers. Left-handers, you will find left-handed charts on page 48 and you will work to the right.

The perfect circle

You will see that the written patterns and charts state the standard chain 3 (starting chain) that traditionally takes the place of the first stitch of the round. That can stand out in a circle and there are 3 options to make your circles appear more seamless.

Option 1

Your first option is to join to just the top strand of your chain 3 starting chain. Doing this makes your chain 3 look more like a real stitch. Why? Well, if you look at a real stitch, the post and the top of the stitch kind of looks like a capital P. (A reverse P if you're left-handed). Joining to just the top strand helps your chain 3 look more like a capital P and has the added bonus of making it really, really easy to see where you work your first real stitch of the next round.

DOT POINT

Don't be concerned how large that loop becomes. When you work your next round of stitches into it, it will all blend in well.

Option 2

Or, if that still stands out too much for you, you can work a false stitch in place of the chain 3 instead. It is fiddly, but I think it is well worth learning. It's how I do it in the videos. It is optional. You don't have to do it if you find it too fiddly or if the chain 3 doesn't stand out for you.

> **Here's how to do it.**
>
> Pull up a long loop, a little taller than a treble/double (UK/US) crochet stitch (A). Place a finger on the loop on the hook and hold it firmly while moving the hook under, and wrapping the long loop around the hook (B). Yarn over and pull that strand under the wrapped long loop (C), yarn over again and pull through all remaining loops on the hook (D). It may look a little strange, but once you work the next stitches of the round, it will blend in nicely. At the end of the round, when it's time to join, you can join under 2 loops, just as if you were working into a regular stitch (E).

DOT POINT

Count your stitches before you join the round! It's much easier.

Option 3

If you want a truly perfect circle, you can work an invisible join in the last round of your circles.

If working an invisible join, you will need to make the chain 3 starting chain and not the false stitch. This is because the starting chain together with the invisible join best mimics a stitch.

I didn't do this, but I wanted to mention it. You'll find information about making invisible joins on the Helpful links page.

DOT POINT

If you have trouble identifying the first stitch of a round when it's time to join, try popping a stitch marker in the first stitch of each round as you make it. Then there will be no doubt when you finish the round where to join.

DOT POINT

Get into the habit of checking your stitch count at the end of making your circles. The squaring off won't work if you don't have the right number of stitches in your circles.

How to attach a new colour

The best way to attach a new colour is to work a real stitch from the very beginning. And, luckily, there is a really easy way to do this.

It's called a standing stitch. All you do is attach your new coloured yarn to your hook with a slip knot, hold that slip knot as you make the required stitch, so you don't lose your yarn over. I show how to do it in the videos.

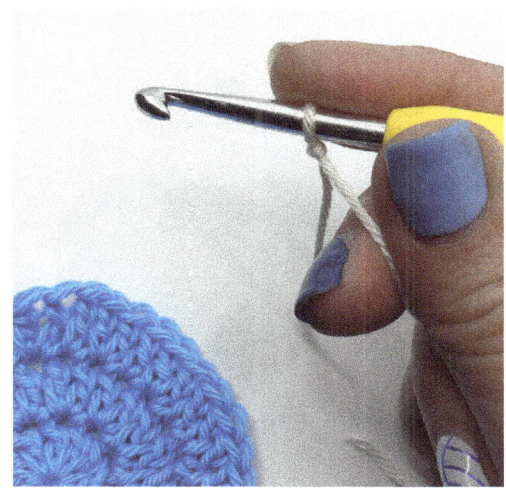

Where to attach your new colour?

It's best to attach your new colour in a place other than where you ended the last colour. It helps make the start and end of rounds blend in. You will see me doing this in the videos.

DOT POINT

Pop a stitch marker in the stitch where you ended the last colour and one in the last stitch made before you joined. This will help you identify where to work stitches when you get to the join.

It can be easy to be fooled into thinking you need to work a stitch into the slip stitch join. These stitch markers make you stop and really look where to work your stitches at that point. This does not apply if you do invisible joins.

The stitch markers show where to work stitches. The needle is pointing to the slip stitch that you ignore.

Seamless Corners

Once you start to square off your dots, you will begin each round with half of a corner. You finish that first corner at the end of the round.

You may be used to chaining the same number of chains as in other corners and then joining with a slip stitch to finish a round. I don't do that. Instead, I have you chain 1 and join with a stitch. Doing this places your hook and yarn in exactly the right spot to begin your next round. There is no need to slip stitch to the right space. It gives you a much more seamless look with no visible line of round joins.

After the first squaring off round, the pattern instructs you to work a stitch over the joining stitch. Treat the joining stitch as a chain space and work your stitch completely over that joining stitch – not into it. The needle in the photo shows where to poke your hook.

Small stitch rounds

When working your small stitch rounds, it can be a bit hard to see what's happening in that first corner. I recommend you pop a scrap of yarn in the gap before you join the small stitch round. That yarn scrap will show you where to put your hook to make the first stitch over the joining stitch and also the last stitch of the round.

DOT POINT

The very last round of every square ends with chain 2 and a slip stitch join as there is no need to end in the middle of a corner.

Joining

I have used my favourite method to join the Dotty Spotty squares.

Here's how to do it.

Hold squares right sides together, attach joining yarn with a standing double crochet (UK)/single crochet (US) to both 2-chain corner spaces of each square at the same time. Work a stitch into both loops of both squares all the way along, end with a stitch in both 2-chain corner spaces. Fasten off.

Here's a little table of the stitch counts for each of the 5 squares.

Pattern	Stitch Count
1 Round Dot	24
2 Round Dot	23
3 Round Dot	22
4 Round Dot	23
5 Round Dot	24

DOT POINT

The slightly different stitch counts are easy to deal with as you join by using the same stitch twice on the smaller stitch count square while using separate stitches on the larger stitch count square. See the squaring off video at 8:45 for a demonstration.

There will be times when the stitch counts do match up, depending on your layout.

DOT POINT

To see a way you can join your squares as you go, watch the squaring off video at 7:30.

Borders

I have included a different border for each of the samples made. You can choose which one you want to add to your blankets.

If you find your border corners are developing a bit of a swirl, skip the first stitch of the side after the corners to straighten it out. The following photos show this in action. The needle is in the stitch to skip.

DOT POINT

If your crab stitch is distorting your edge, try using a smaller hook so it doesn't get too wavy.

Blocking

To make your Dotty Spotty creations sing, I recommend blocking your squares and blankets.

> Here's how I do it.
>
> Pin your squares out on a foam mat or folded towel. Squirt it with steam from your iron. Once the squares are cool and dry, the job is done.
>
> I steamed the edges of my blankets the same way.

DOT POINT

If you use wool, you may need to wet block for the best results. Wash your blanket per your yarn label instructions and pin out to dry.

THE PATTERNS

1 Round Dot

UK Terms

Using Dot Colour, begin with mc.

R1: ch3 (stch), 11tr, join with ss to 3rd ch of stch. Fasten off. {12 sts}

R2: Attach Parchment with stdg tr to any st, tr in same st, *htr in next 2 sts**,(2tr, ch2, 2tr) in next st*, rep from * to * 2x and * to ** 1x, 2tr in same st as first sts, ch1, join with dc to first st.
{6 sts on each side; 4 2-ch cnr sps}

R3: ch3 (stch), tr over joining dc, *tr in next 6 sts**, (2tr, ch2, 2tr) in 2-ch cnr sp*, rep from * to * 2x and * to ** 1x, 2tr in same sp as first sts, ch1, join with dc to 3rd ch of stch.
{10 sts on each side; 4 2-ch cnr sps}

R4: ch3 (stch), tr over joining dc, *tr in next 10 sts**, (2tr, ch2, 2tr) in 2-ch cnr sp*, rep from * to * 2x and * to ** 1x, 2tr in same sp as first sts, ch1, join with dc to 3rd ch of stch.
{14 sts on each side; 4 2-ch cnr sps}

R5: ch3 (stch), tr over joining dc, *tr in next 14 sts**, (2tr, ch2, 2tr) in 2-ch cnr sp*, rep from * to * 2x and * to ** 1x, 2tr in same sp first sts, ch1, join with dc to 3rd ch of stch.
{18 sts on each side; 4 2-ch cnr sps}

R6: ch3 (stch), tr over joining dc, *tr in next 18 sts**, (2tr, ch2, 2tr) in 2-ch cnr sp*, rep from * to * 2x and * to ** 1x, 2tr in same sp as first sts, ch1, join with dc to 3rd ch of stch.
{22 sts on each side; 4 2-ch cnr sps}

R7: dc over joining dc, *dc in next 22 sts**, (dc, ch2, dc) in 2-ch cnr sp*, rep from * to * 2x and * to ** 1x, dc in same sp as first st, ch2, join with ss to first st. Fasten off.
{24 sts on each side; 4 2-ch cnr sps}

US Terms

Using Dot Colour, begin with mc.

R1: ch3 (stch), 11dc, join with ss to 3rd ch of stch. Fasten off. {12 sts}

R2: Attach Parchment with stdg dc to any st, dc in same st, *hdc in next 2 sts**,(2dc, ch2, 2dc) in next st*, rep from * to * 2x and * to ** 1x, 2dc in same st as first sts, ch1, join with sc to first st. {6 sts on each side; 4 2-ch cnr sps}

R3: ch3 (stch), dc over joining sc, *dc in next 6 sts**, (2dc, ch2, 2dc) in 2-ch cnr sp*, rep from * to * 2x and * to ** 1x, 2dc in same sp as first sts, ch1, join with sc to 3rd ch of stch. {10 sts on each side; 4 2-ch cnr sps}

R4: ch3 (stch), dc over joining sc, *dc in next 10 sts**, (2dc, ch2, 2dc) in 2-ch cnr sp*, rep from * to * 2x and * to ** 1x, 2dc in same sp as first sts, ch1, join with sc to 3rd ch of stch. {14 sts on each side; 4 2-ch cnr sps}

R5: ch3 (stch), dc over joining sc, *dc in next 14 sts**, (2dc, ch2, 2dc) in 2-ch cnr sp*, rep from * to * 2x and * to ** 1x, 2dc in same sp first sts, ch1, join with sc to 3rd ch of stch. {18 sts on each side; 4 2-ch cnr sps}

R6: ch3 (stch), dc over joining sc, *dc in next 18 sts**, (2dc, ch2, 2dc) in 2-ch cnr sp*, rep from * to * 2x and * to ** 1x, 2dc in same sp as first sts, ch1, join with sc to 3rd ch of stch. {22 sts on each side; 4 2-ch cnr sps}

R7: sc over joining sc, *sc in next 22 sts**, (sc, ch2, sc) in 2-ch cnr sp*, rep from * to * 2x and * to ** 1x, sc in same sp as first st, ch2, join with ss to first st. Fasten off. {24 sts on each side; 4 2-ch cnr sps}

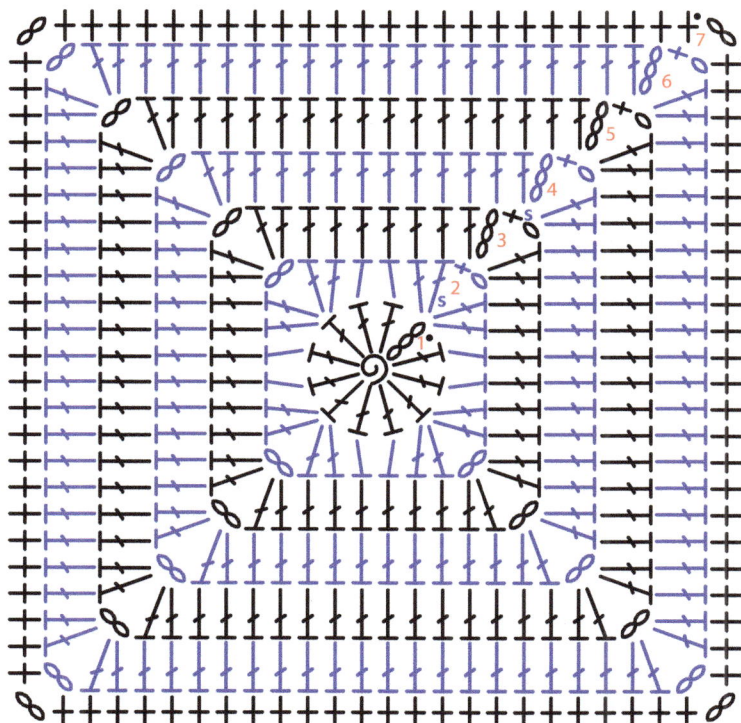

2 Round Dot

UK Terms

Using Dot Colour, begin with mc.

R1: ch3 (stch), 11tr, join with ss to 3rd ch of stch. {12 sts}

R2: ch3 (stch), tr in same st as ss, 2tr in next 11 sts, join with ss to 3rd ch of stch. Fasten off. {24 sts}

R3: Attach Parchment with stdg dtr to any st, tr in same st, *tr in next st, htr in next st, dc in next st, htr in next st, tr in next st**, (tr, dtr, ch2, dtr, tr) in next st*, rep from * to * 2x and * to ** 1x, (tr, dtr) in same st as first sts, ch1, join with dc to first st. {9 sts on each side; 4 2-ch cnr sps}

R4: ch3 (stch), tr over joining dc, *tr in next 9 sts**, (2tr, ch2, 2tr) in 2-ch cnr sp*, rep from * to * 2x and * to ** 1x, 2tr in same sp as first sts, ch1, join with dc to 3rd ch of stch.
{13 sts on each side; 4 2-ch cnr sps}

R5: ch3 (stch), tr over joining dc, *tr in next 13 sts**, (2tr, ch2, 2tr) in 2-ch cnr sp*, rep from * to * 2x and * to ** 1x, 2tr in same sp as first sts, ch1, join with dc to 3rd ch of stch.
{17 sts on each side; 4 2-ch cnr sps}

R6: ch3 (stch), tr over joining dc, *tr in next 17 sts**, (2tr, ch2, 2tr) in 2-ch sp*, rep from * to * 2x and * to ** 1x, 2tr in same sp as first sts, ch1, join with dc to 3rd ch of stch.
{21 sts on each side; 4 2-ch cnr sps}

R7: dc over joining dc, *dc in next 21 sts**, (dc, ch2, dc) in 2-ch cnr sp*, rep from * to * 2x and * to ** 1x, 2dc in same sp as first st, ch2, join with ss to first st. Fasten off.
{23 sts on each side; 4 2-ch cnr sps}

US Terms

Using Dot Colour, begin with mc.

R1: ch3 (stch), 11dc, join with ss to 3rd ch of stch. {12 sts}

R2: ch3 (stch), dc in same st as ss, 2dc in next 11 sts, join with ss to 3rd ch of stch. Fasten off. {24 sts}

R3: Attach Parchment with stdg tr to any st, dc in same st, *dc in next st, hdc in next st, sc in next st, hdc in next st, dc in next st**, (dc, tr, ch2, tr, dc) in next st*, rep from * to * 2x and * to ** 1x, (dc, tr) in same st as first sts, ch1, join with sc to first st. {9 sts on each side; 4 2-ch cnr sps}

R4: ch3 (stch), dc over joining sc, *dc in next 9 sts**, (2dc, ch2, 2dc) in 2-ch cnr sp*, rep from * to * 2x and * to ** 1x, 2dc in same sp as first sts, ch1, join with sc to 3rd ch of stch. {13 sts on each side; 4 2-ch cnr sps}

R5: ch3 (stch), dc over joining sc, *dc in next 13 sts**, (2dc, ch2, 2dc) in 2-ch cnr sp*, rep from * to * 2x and * to ** 1x, 2dc in same sp as first sts, ch1, join with sc to 3rd ch of stch. {17 sts on each side; 4 2-ch cnr sps}

R6: ch3 (stch), dc over joining sc, *dc in next 17 sts**, (2dc, ch2, 2dc) in 2-ch sp*, rep from * to * 2x and * to ** 1x, 2dc in same sp as first sts, ch1, join with sc to 3rd ch of stch. {21 sts on each side; 4 2-ch cnr sps}

R7: sc over joining sc, *sc in next 21 sts**, (sc, ch2, sc) in 2-ch cnr sp*, rep from * to * 2x and * to ** 1x, 2sc in same sp as first st, ch2, join with ss to first st. Fasten off. {23 sts on each side; 4 2-ch cnr sps}

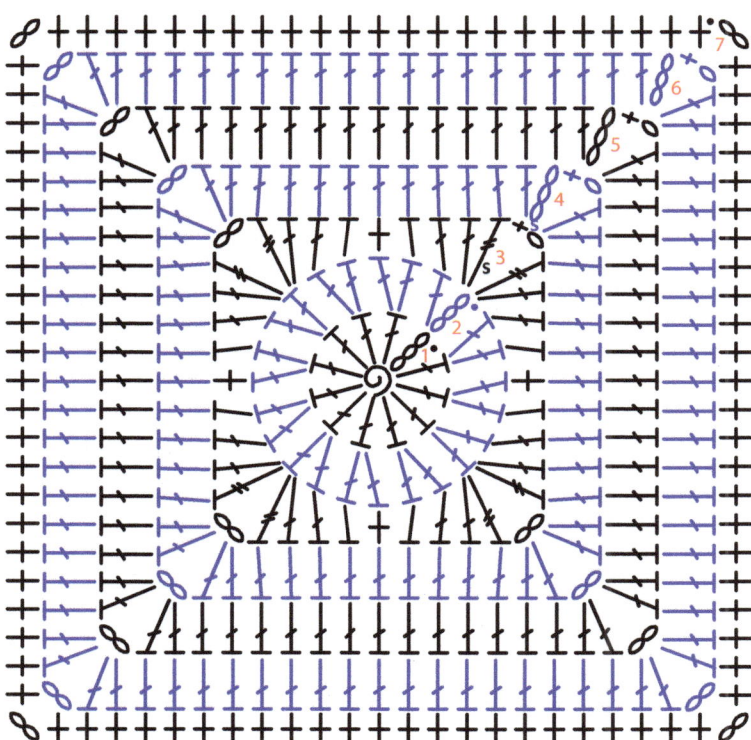

25

3 Round Dot

UK Terms

Using Dot Colour, begin with mc.

R1: ch3 (stch), 11tr, join with ss to 3rd ch of stch. {12 sts}

R2: ch3 (stch), tr in same st as ss, 2tr in next 11 sts, join with ss to 3rd ch of stch. {24 sts}

R3: ch3 (stch), tr in same st as ss, *tr in next st**, 2tr in next st*, rep from * to * 10x and * to ** 1x, join with ss to 3rd ch of stch. Fasten off. {36 sts}

R4: Attach Parchment with stdg dtr to any st, dtr in same st, *tr in next st, htr in next 2 sts, dc in next 2 sts, htr in next 2 sts, tr in next st**, (2dtr, ch2, 2dtr) in next st*, rep from * to * 2x and * to ** 1x, 2dtr in same st as first sts, ch1, join with dc to first st. {12 sts on each side; 4 2-ch cnr sps}

R5: ch3 (stch), tr over joining dc, *tr in next 12 sts**, (2tr, ch2, 2tr) in 2-ch cnr sp*, rep from * to * 2x and * to ** 1x, 2tr in same sp first sts, ch1, join with dc to 3rd ch of stch.
{16 sts on each side; 4 2-ch cnr sps}

R6: ch3 (stch), tr over joining dc, *tr in next 16 sts**, (2tr, ch2, 2tr) in 2-ch cnr sp*, rep from * to * 2x and * to ** 1x, 2tr in same sp first sts, ch1, join with dc to 3rd ch of stch.
{20 sts on each side; 4 2-ch cnr sps}

R7: dc over joining dc, *dc in next 20 sts**, (dc, ch2, dc) in 2-ch cnr sp*, rep from * to * 2x and * to ** 1x, dc in same sp as first st, ch2, join with ss to first st. Fasten off.
{22 sts on each side; 4 2-ch cnr sps}

US Terms

Using Dot Colour, begin with mc.

R1: ch3 (stch), 11dc, join with ss to 3rd ch of stch. {12 sts}

R2: ch3 (stch), dc in same st as ss, 2dc in next 11 sts, join with ss to 3rd ch of stch. {24 sts}

R3: ch3 (stch), dc in same st as ss, *dc in next st**, 2dc in next st*, rep from * to * 10x and * to ** 1x, join with ss to 3rd ch of stch. Fasten off. {36 sts}

R4: Attach Parchment with stdg tr to any st, tr in same st, *dc in next st, hdc in next 2 sts, sc in next 2 sts, hdc in next 2 sts, dc in next st**, (2tr, ch2, 2tr) in next st*, rep from * to * 2x and * to ** 1x, 2tr in same st as first sts, ch1, join with sc to first st. {12 sts on each side; 4 2-ch cnr sps}

R5: ch3 (stch), dc over joining sc, *dc in next 12 sts**, (2dc, ch2, 2dc) in 2-ch cnr sp*, rep from * to * 2x and * to ** 1x, 2dc in same sp first sts, ch1, join with sc to 3rd ch of stch. {16 sts on each side; 4 2-ch cnr sps}

R6: ch3 (stch), dc over joining sc, *dc in next 16 sts**, (2dc, ch2, 2dc) in 2-ch cnr sp*, rep from * to * 2x and * to ** 1x, 2dc in same sp first sts, ch1, join with sc to 3rd ch of stch. {20 sts on each side; 4 2-ch cnr sps}

R7: sc over joining sc, *sc in next 20 sts**, (sc, ch2, sc) in 2-ch cnr sp*, rep from * to * 2x and * to ** 1x, sc in same sp as first st, ch2, join with ss to first st. Fasten off. {22 sts on each side; 4 2-ch cnr sps}

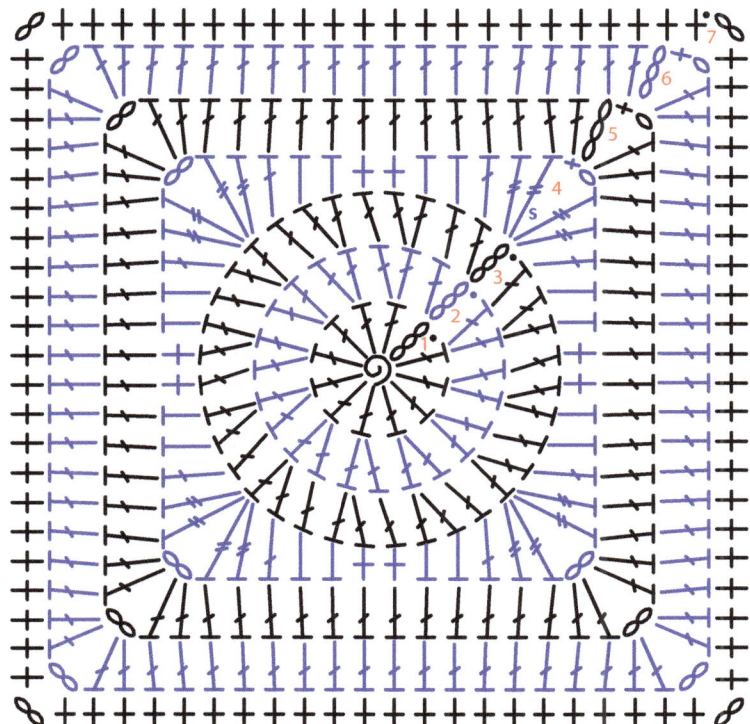

4 Round Dot

UK Terms

Using Dot Colour, begin with mc.

R1: ch3 (stch), 11tr, join with ss to 3rd ch of stch. {12sts}

R2: ch3 (stch), tr in same st as ss, 2tr in next 11 sts, join with ss to 3rd ch of stch. {24 sts}

R3: ch3 (stch), tr in same st as ss, *tr in next st**, 2tr in next st*, rep from * to * 10x and * to ** 1x, join with ss to 3rd ch of stch. {36 sts}

R4: ch3 (stch), tr in same st as ss, *tr in next 2 sts**, 2tr in next st*, rep from * to * 10x and * to ** 1x, join with ss to 3rd ch of stch. Fasten off. {48 sts}

R5: Attach Parchment with stdg dtr to any st, dtr in same st, *tr in next 2 sts, htr in next 2 sts, dc in next 3 sts, htr in next 2 sts, tr in next 2 sts**, (2dtr, ch2, 2dtr) in next st*, rep from * to * 2x and * to ** 1x, 2dtr in same st as first sts, ch1, join with dc to first st.
{15 sts on each side; 4 2-ch cnr sps}

R6: ch3 (stch), tr over joining dc, *tr in next 15 sts**, (2tr, ch2, 2tr) in 2-ch cnr sp*, rep from * to * 2x and * to ** 1x, 2tr in same sp as first sts, ch1, join with dc to 3rd ch of stch.
{19 sts on each side; 4 2-ch cnr sps}

R7: dc over joining dc, *dc in next 19 sts**, (dc, ch2, dc) in 2-ch cnr sp*, rep from * to * 2x and * to ** 1x, dc in same sp as first st, ch1, join with dc to first dc. {21 sts on each side; 4 2-ch cnr sps}

R8: dc over joining dc, *dc in next 21 sts**, (dc, ch2, dc) in 2-ch cnr sp*, rep from * to * 2x and * to ** 1x, dc in same sp as first st, ch2, join with ss to first st. Fasten off.
{23 sts on each side; 4 2-ch cnr sps}

US Terms

Using Dot Colour, begin with mc.

R1: ch3 (stch), 11dc, join with ss to 3rd ch of stch. {12sts}

R2: ch3 (stch), dc in same st as ss, 2dc in next 11 sts, join with ss to 3rd ch of stch. {24 sts}

R3: ch3 (stch), dc in same st as ss, *dc in next st**, 2dc in next st*, rep from * to * 10x and * to ** 1x, join with ss to 3rd ch of stch. {36 sts}

R4: ch3 (stch), dc in same st as ss, *dc in next 2 sts**, 2dc in next st*, rep from * to * 10x and * to ** 1x, join with ss to 3rd ch of stch. Fasten off. {48 sts}

R5: Attach Parchment with stdg tr to any st, tr in same st, *dc in next 2 sts, hdc in next 2 sts, sc in next 3 sts, hdc in next 2 sts, dc in next 2 sts**, (2tr, ch2, 2tr) in next st*, rep from * to * 2x and * to ** 1x, 2tr in same st as first sts, ch1, join with sc to first st. {15 sts on each side; 4 2-ch cnr sps}

R6: ch3 (stch), dc over joining sc, *dc in next 15 sts**, (2dc, ch2, 2dc) in 2-ch cnr sp*, rep from * to * 2x and * to ** 1x, 2dc in same sp as first sts, ch1, join with sc to 3rd ch of stch. {19 sts on each side; 4 2-ch cnr sps}

R7: sc over joining sc, *sc in next 19 sts**, (sc, ch2, sc) in 2-ch cnr sp*, rep from * to * 2x and * to ** 1x, sc in same sp as first st, ch1, join with sc to first sc. {21 sts on each side; 4 2-ch cnr sps}

R8: sc over joining sc, *sc in next 21 sts**, (sc, ch2, sc) in 2-ch cnr sp*, rep from * to * 2x and * to ** 1x, sc in same sp as first st, ch2, join with ss to first st. Fasten off. {23 sts on each side; 4 2-ch cnr sps}

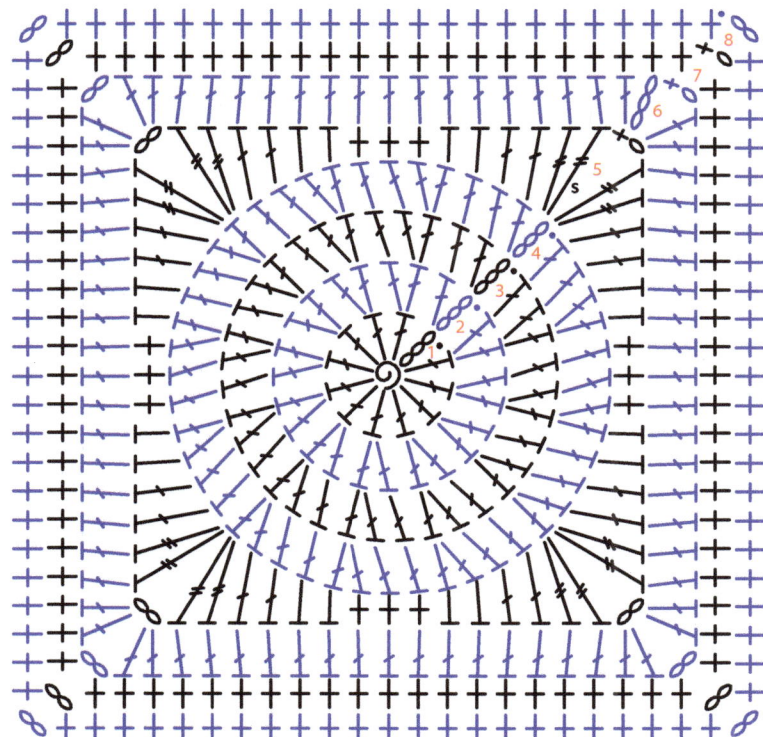

5 Round Dot

UK Terms

Using Dot Colour, begin with mc.

R1: ch3 (stch), 11tr, join with ss to 3rd ch of stch. {12 sts}

R2: ch3 (stch), tr in same st as ss, 2tr in next 11 sts, join with ss to 3rd ch of stch. {24 sts}

R3: ch3 (stch), tr in same st as ss, *tr in next st**, 2tr in next st*, rep from * to * 10x and * to ** 1x, join with ss to 3rd ch of stch. {36 sts}

R4: ch3 (stch), tr in same st as ss, *tr in next 2 sts**, 2tr in next st*, rep from * to * 10x and * to ** 1x, join with ss to 3rd ch of stch. {48 sts}

R5: ch3 (stch), tr in same st as ss, *tr in next 3 sts**, 2tr in next st*, rep from * to * 10x and * to ** 1x, join with ss to 3rd ch of stch. Fasten off. {60 sts}

R6: Attach Parchment with stdg dtr to any st, dtr in same st, *tr in next 3 sts, htr in next 3 sts, dc in next 2 sts, htr in next 3 sts, tr in next 3 sts**, (2dtr, ch2, 2dtr) in next st*, rep from * to * 2x and * to ** 1x, 2dtr in same st as first sts, ch1, join with dc to first st.
{18 sts on each side; 4 2-ch cnr sps}

R7: 2dc over joining dc, *dc in next 18 sts**, (2dc, ch2, 2dc) in 2-ch cnr sp*, rep from * to * 2x and * to ** 1x, 2dc in same sp as first sts, ch1, join with dc to first st.
{22 sts on each side; 4 2-ch cnr sps}

R8: dc over joining dc, *dc in next 22 sts**, (dc, ch2, dc) in 2-ch cnr sp*, rep from * to * 2x and * to ** 1x, dc in same sp as first st, ch2, join with ss to first st. Fasten off.
{24 sts on each side; 4 2-ch cnr sps}

US Terms

Using Dot Colour, begin with mc.

R1: ch3 (stch), 11dc, join with ss to 3rd ch of stch. {12 sts}

R2: ch3 (stch), dc in same st as ss, 2dc in next 11 sts, join with ss to 3rd ch of stch. {24 sts}

R3: ch3 (stch), dc in same st as ss, *dc in next st**, 2dc in next st*, rep from * to * 10x and * to ** 1x, join with ss to 3rd ch of stch. {36 sts}

R4: ch3 (stch), dc in same st as ss, *dc in next 2 sts**, 2dc in next st*, rep from * to * 10x and * to ** 1x, join with ss to 3rd ch of stch. {48 sts}

R5: ch3 (stch), dc in same st as ss, *dc in next 3 sts**, 2dc in next st*, rep from * to * 10x and * to ** 1x, join with ss to 3rd ch of stch. Fasten off. {60 sts}

R6: Attach Parchment with stdg tr to any st, tr in same st, *dc in next 3 sts, hdc in next 3 sts, sc in next 2 sts, hdc in next 3 sts, dc in next 3 sts**, (2tr, ch2, 2tr) in next st*, rep from * to * 2x and * to ** 1x, 2tr in same st as first sts, ch1, join with sc to first st. {18 sts on each side; 4 2-ch cnr sps}

R7: 2sc over joining sc, *sc in next 18 sts**, (2sc, ch2, 2sc) in 2-ch cnr sp*, rep from * to * 2x and * to ** 1x, 2sc in same sp as first sts, ch1, join with sc to first st. {22 sts on each side; 4 2-ch cnr sps}

R8: sc over joining sc, *sc in next 22 sts**, (sc, ch2, sc) in 2-ch cnr sp*, rep from * to * 2x and * to ** 1x, sc in same sp as first st, ch2, join with ss to first st. Fasten off. {24 sts on each side; 4 2-ch cnr sps}

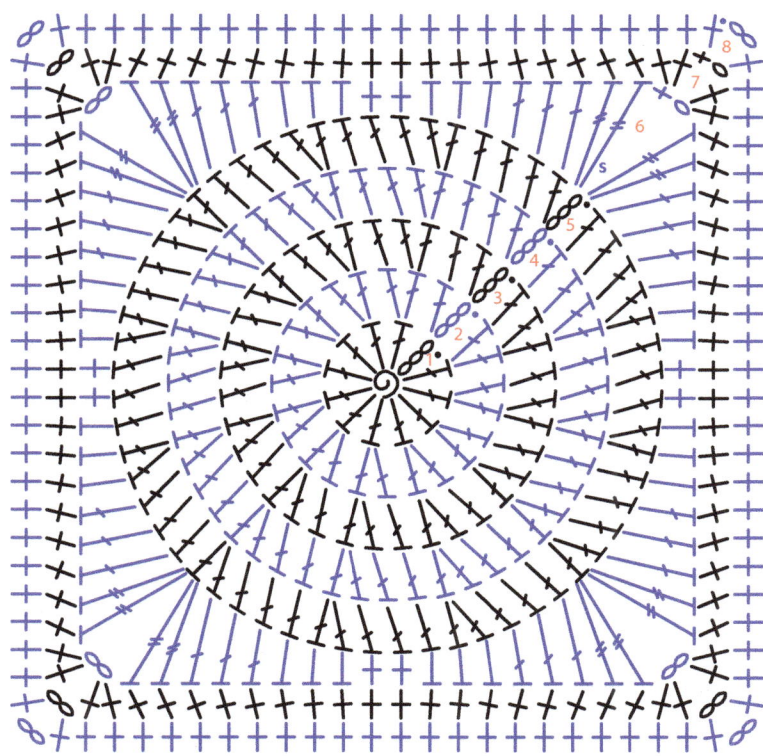

BLANKET INSTRUCTIONS

The Original Dotty Spotty Baby Blanket

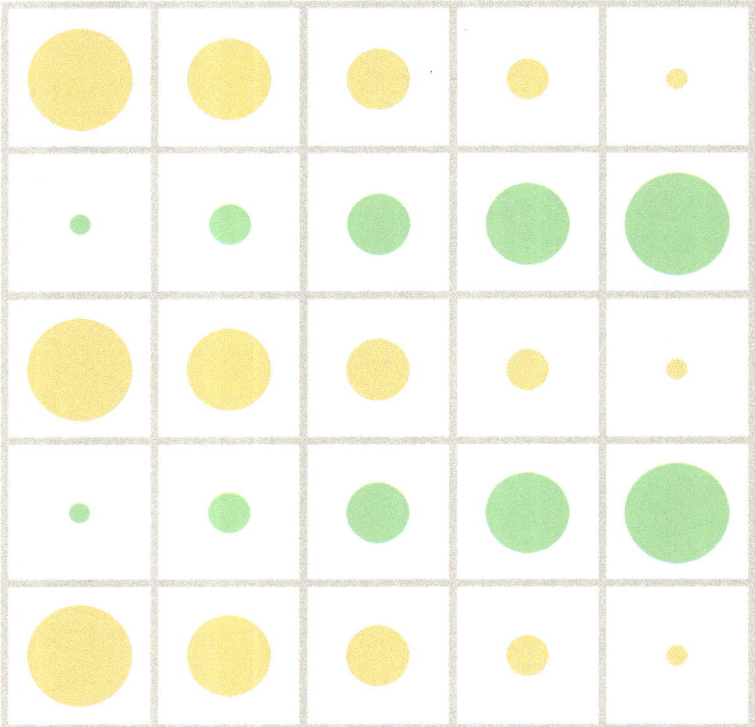

	🟡	🟢
1 Round Dot	3	2
2 Round Dot	3	2
3 Round Dot	3	2
4 Round Dot	3	2
5 Round Dot	3	2

Make all 25 squares and join them as shown, then add the following border.

Border pattern

UK Terms

R1: Attach Neutral with a stdg dc to any 2-ch cnr sp, *dc in each st on side, working a dc in each 2-ch sp and join**, (dc, ch2, dc) in 2-ch cnr sp*, rep from * to * 2x and * to ** 1x, dc in same sp as first st, ch1, join with dc to first st.

R2: dc over joining dc, *dc in each st on side**, (dc, ch2, dc) in 2-ch cnr sp*, rep from * to * 2x & * to ** 1x, dc in same sp as first st, ch2, join with ss to first st. Fasten off.

R3: Attach Green with a stdg dc to any 2-ch cnr sp, *dc in each st on side**, (dc, ch2, dc) in 2-ch cnr sp*, rep from * to * 2x & * to ** 1x, dc in same sp as first st, ch1, join with dc to first st.

R4: dc over joining dc, *dc in each st on side**, (dc, ch2, dc) in 2-ch cnr sp*, rep from * to * 2x & * to ** 1x, dc in same sp as first st, ch2, join with ss to first st. Fasten off.

R5 & R6: Rep R3 & R4 with Neutral.

R7 & R8: Rep R3 & R4 with Yellow.

US Terms

R1: Attach Neutral with a stdg sc to any 2-ch cnr sp, *sc in each st on side, working a sc in each 2-ch sp and join**, (sc, ch2, sc) in 2-ch cnr sp*, rep from * to * 2x and * to ** 1x, sc in same sp as first st, ch1, join with sc to first st.

R2: sc over joining sc, *sc in each st on side**, (sc, ch2, sc) in 2-ch cnr sp*, rep from * to * 2x & * to ** 1x, sc in same sp as first st, ch2, join with ss to first st. Fasten off.

R3: Attach Green with a stdg sc to any 2-ch cnr sp, *sc in each st on side**, (sc, ch2, sc) in 2-ch cnr sp*, rep from * to * 2x & * to ** 1x, sc in same sp as first st, ch1, join with sc to first st.

R4: sc over joining sc, *sc in each st on side**, (sc, ch2, sc) in 2-ch cnr sp*, rep from * to * 2x & * to ** 1x, sc in same sp as first st, ch2, join with ss to first st. Fasten off.

R5 & R6: Rep R3 & R4 with Neutral.

R7 & R8: Rep R3 & R4 with Yellow.

The Random Dotty Spotty Baby Blanket

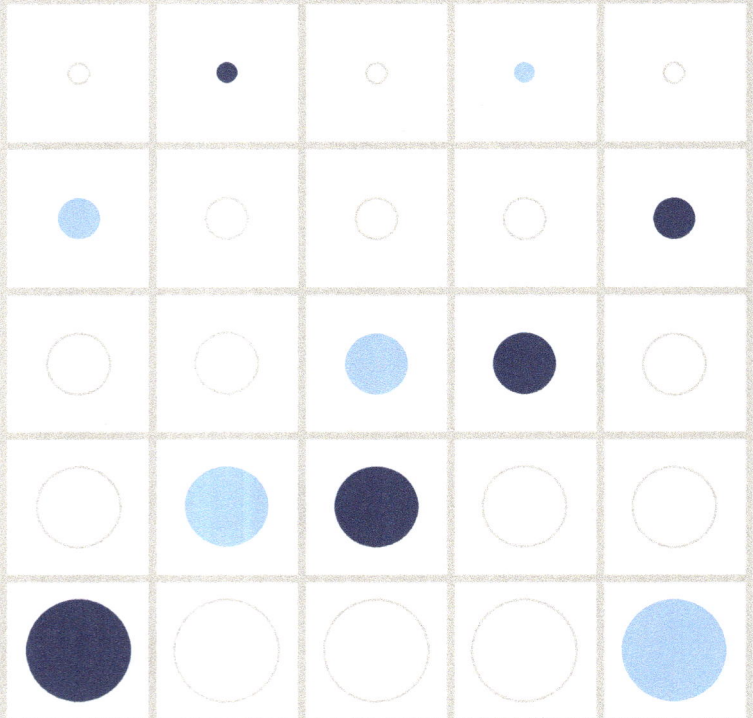

	●	●	○
1 Round Dot	1	1	3
2 Round Dot	1	1	3
3 Round Dot	1	1	3
4 Round Dot	1	1	3
5 Round Dot	1	1	3

Make all 25 squares and join them as shown, then add the following border.

Border pattern

UK Terms

R1: Attach White with a stdg dc to any 2-ch cnr sp, *dc in each st on side, working a dc in each 2-ch sp and join**, (dc, ch2, dc) in 2-ch cnr sp*, rep from * to * 2x and * to ** 1x, dc in same sp as first st, ch1, join with dc to first st.

R2: dc over joining dc, *dc in each st on side**, (dc, ch2, dc) in 2-ch cnr sp*, rep from * to * 2x & * to ** 1x, dc in same sp as first st, ch1, join with dc to first st.

R3: Rep R2.

R4: ch3 (stch), *tr in each st on side**, (tr, ch2, tr) in 2-ch cnr sp*, rep from * to * 2x & * to ** 1x, tr in same sp as first st, ch1, join with dc to 3rd ch of stch.

R5: Rep R2.

R6: crab st in corner sp, *crab st in each st on side**, crab st in 2-ch cnr sp*, rep from * to * 2x & * to ** 1x, join with ss to first st. Fasten off.

US Terms

R1: Attach White with a stdg sc to any 2-ch cnr sp, *sc in each st on side, working a sc in each 2-ch sp and join**, (sc, ch2, sc) in 2-ch cnr sp*, rep from * to * 2x and * to ** 1x, sc in same sp as first st, ch1, join with sc to first st.

R2: sc over joining sc, *sc in each st on side**, (sc, ch2, sc) in 2-ch cnr sp*, rep from * to * 2x & * to ** 1x, sc in same sp as first st, ch1, join with sc to first st.

R3: Rep R2.

R4: ch3 (stch), *dc in each st on side**, (dc, ch2, dc) in 2-ch cnr sp*, rep from * to * 2x & * to ** 1x, dc in same sp as first st, ch1, join with sc to 3rd ch of stch.

R5: Rep R2.

R6: crab st in corner sp, *crab st in each st on side**, crab st in 2-ch cnr sp*, rep from * to * 2x & * to ** 1x, join with ss to first st. Fasten off.

The Dotty Spotty Big Kid Blanket

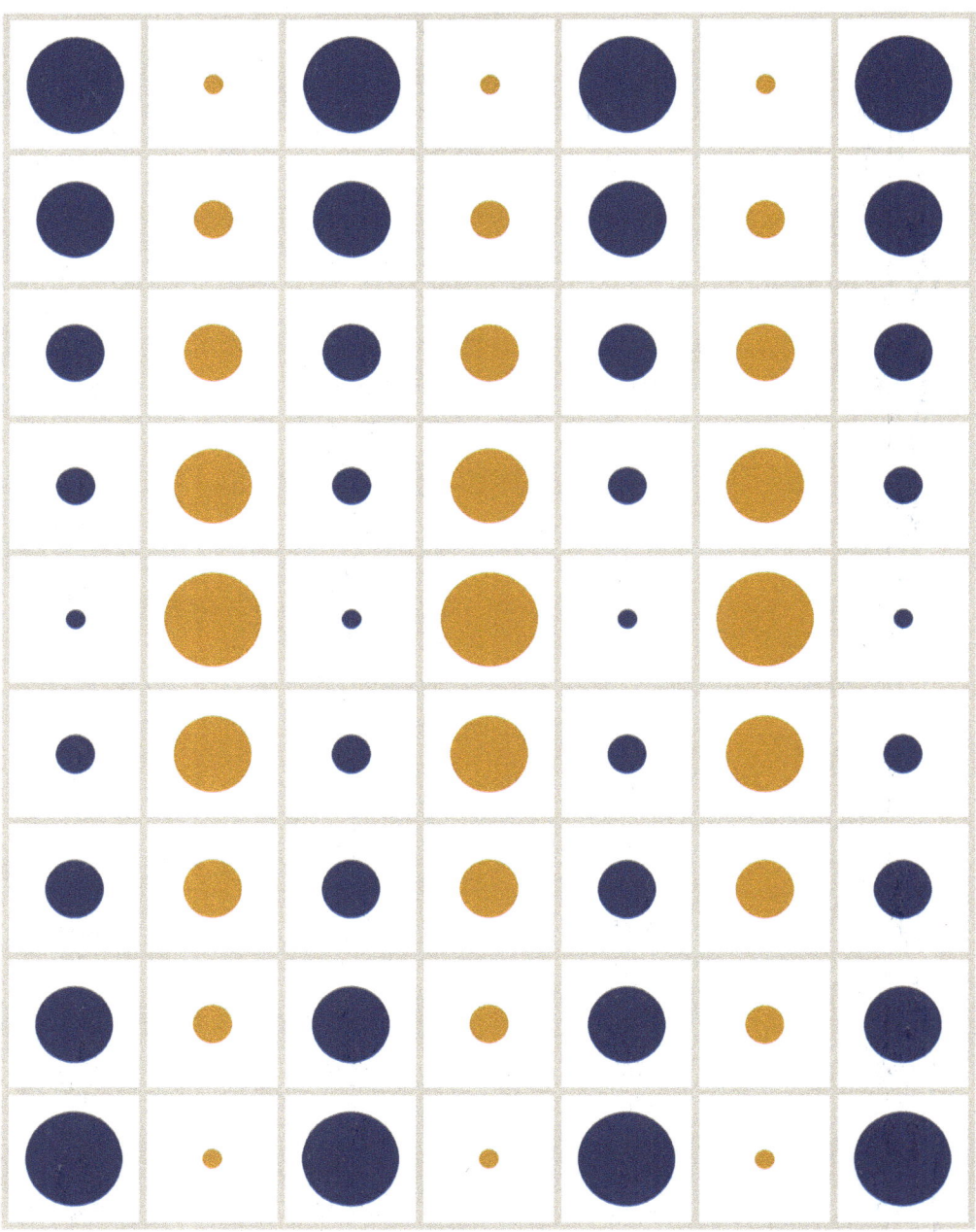

36

	🟡	🔵
1 Round Dot	6	4
2 Round Dot	6	8
3 Round Dot	6	8
4 Round Dot	6	8
5 Round Dot	3	8

Make all 63 squares and join them as shown, then add the following border.

UK Terms

R1: Attach Neutral with a stdg dc to any 2-ch cnr sp, *dc in each st on side, working a dc in each 2-ch sp and join**, (dc, ch2, dc) in 2-ch cnr sp*, rep from * to * 2x and * to ** 1x, dc in same sp as first st, ch1, join with dc to first st.

R2: dc over joining dc, *dc in each st on side**, (dc, ch2, dc) in 2-ch cnr sp*, rep from * to * 2x & * to ** 1x, dc in same sp as first st, ch2, join with ss to first st. Fasten off.

R3: Attach Mustard with a stdg dc to any 2-ch cnr sp, *dc in each st on side**, (dc, ch2, dc) in 2-ch cnr sp*, rep from * to * 2x & * to ** 1x, dc in same sp as first st, ch1, join with dc to first st.

R4: dc over joining dc, *dc in each st on side**, (dc, ch2, dc) in 2-ch cnr sp*, rep from * to * 2x & * to ** 1x, dc in same sp as first st, ch2, join with ss to first st. Fasten off.

R5 & R6: Rep R3 & R4 with Navy.

R7: Rep R3 with Neutral.

R8: dc over joining dc, *dc in each st on side**, (dc, ch2, dc) in 2-ch cnr sp*, rep from * to * 2x & * to ** 1x, dc in same sp as first st, ch1, join with dc to first st.

R9: Rep R8 with Neutral.

R10: Rep R4.

US Terms

R1: Attach Neutral with a stdg sc to any 2-ch cnr sp, *sc in each st on side, working a sc in each 2-ch sp and join**, (sc, ch2, sc) in 2-ch cnr sp*, rep from * to * 2x and * to ** 1x, sc in same sp as first st, ch1, join with sc to first st.

R2: sc over joining sc, *sc in each st on side**, (sc, ch2, sc) in 2-ch cnr sp*, rep from * to * 2x & * to ** 1x, sc in same sp as first st, ch2, join with ss to first st. Fasten off.

R3: Attach Mustard with a stdg sc to any 2-ch cnr sp, *sc in each st on side**, (sc, ch2, sc) in 2-ch cnr sp*, rep from * to * 2x & * to ** 1x, sc in same sp as first st, ch1, join with sc to first st.

R4: sc over joining sc, *sc in each st on side**, (sc, ch2, sc) in 2-ch cnr sp*, rep from * to * 2x & * to ** 1x, sc in same sp as first st, ch2, join with ss to first st. Fasten off.

R5 & R6: Rep R3 & R4 with Navy.

R7: Rep R3 with Neutral.

R8: sc over joining sc, *sc in each st on side**, (sc, ch2, sc) in 2-ch cnr sp*, rep from * to * 2x & * to ** 1x, sc in same sp as first st, ch1, join with sc to first st.

R9: Rep R8 with Neutral.

R10: Rep R4.

MAKE IT YOUR OWN

Plan your layout

The samples I made for this book are just the tip of the iceberg when it comes to possible layouts. There are just so many options. Here are just a few other ideas:

- Use only one dot size pattern.
- Use your stash leftovers for the dots in all the colours of the rainbow and square them all off with a solid – light or dark.
- Do a diagonal layout of colours while using the same sized dots.
- Stop at the first squaring off round for a dot pattern for smaller squares.

I am sure you can think of many more!

How to figure out your yarn needs

If you are using a similar yarn to me, use these specs to work out your yarn needs.

Yarn weight & yardage	4 ply/sock/fingering 3.35 metres/3.66 yards per gram
Finished square size	12 cm/4.75 in when made with a 3.5 mm hook

Pattern	Dot *grams used*	Squaring Off *grams used*	One colour complete square *grams used*
1 Round Dot	0.5	8	8.5
2 Round Dot	1	7	8
3 Round Dot	2	6	8
4 Round Dot	3	5.5	8.5
5 Round Dot	4.5	4	8.25

Yarn weight & yardage	8 ply/DK/light worsted 2.43 metres/2.66 yards per gram
Finished Square Size	15 cm/6 in when made with a 4.5 mm hook

Pattern	Dot *grams used*	Squaring Off *grams used*	One colour complete square *grams used*
1 Round Dot	0.75	13	13.75
2 Round Dot	1.75	11.25	13
3 Round Dot	3	9	12
4 Round Dot	4.75	9	13.75
5 Round Dot	7	6	13

Yarn weight & yardage	10 ply/aran/worsted 1.8 metre/1.97 yards per gram
Finished Square Size	18 cm/7 in when made with a 5.5 mm hook

Pattern	Dot *grams used*	Squaring Off *grams used*	One colour complete square *grams used*
1 Round Dot	1	19	20
2 Round Dot	2.5	17	19.5
3 Round Dot	5	14	19
4 Round Dot	7.5	13	20.5
5 Round Dot	11	10	21

DOT POINT

Don't weave in your ends until after you have weighed your dots and squares or you may be short with your calculations.

If your metres/yards per gram is different to that of my yarns, you can work out your yarn needs by making each pattern and weighing them. I've included a worksheet to help you record your calculations on page 44.

Make your dots first and weigh them.

Then square them all off and weigh them as well.

Work out the difference between your square and dot weights for how much yarn the squaring off used.

Plan your layout using the colouring sheet on page 42. If you need more circles, copy the page a couple of times and tape them together.

Write down how many of each pattern and in what colours you plan on making them. Use the figures above to work out how much yarn of each colour you will need.

Joining and border yarn needs

You will need to add extra for joining and the border pattern you choose. The heavier weight of yarn and the larger your blanket, the more you would have to add.

I suggest you add 20-30% of your squaring off colour for joining and the bulk of your border. Once you have all those figures, I would add another 10% just to be sure.

Yarn Needs Worksheet

Project details

Yarn Name: _____

Yarn Weight (4 ply/sock/DK etc): _____

Grams/ounces per ball (A): _____

Hook Size: _____

Pattern	Dot weight (B)	Square weight (C)	Squaring weight (C-B = D)
1 Round Dot			
2 Round Dot			
3 Round Dot			
4 Round Dot			
5 Round Dot			

Project Plan			
Pattern	Number needed (E)	Needed for Dots (ExB=F)	Needed for Squaring (ExD=G)
1 Round Dot			
2 Round Dot			
3 Round Dot			
4 Round Dot			
5 Round Dot			
TOTAL		=H	=I

Yarn needed – repeat for each colour as needed		
Colour	Total Weight	Number of Balls needed
Dots Colour	H	=H÷A
Squaring Colour	I + 20 to 30% for joining and border (=J)	=J÷A

DOTTY SPOTTY BLANKET COLOURING SHEET

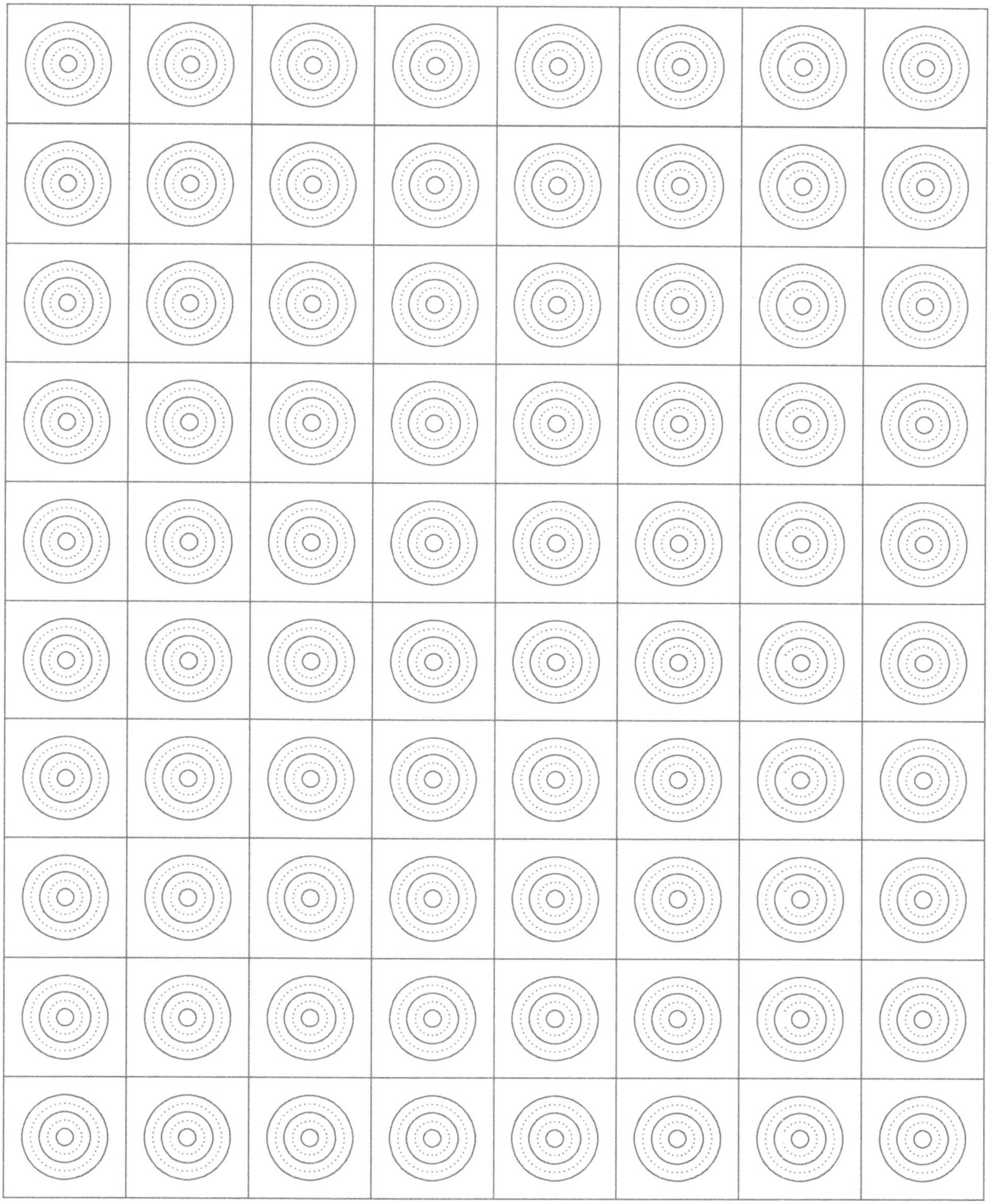

NOTES

45

GLOSSARY

Abbreviations			
	cnr/s	corner/s	
	mc	magic circle	Method used to begin a square. Wrap yarn around a few fingers, forming a loop, insert your hook into the centre and pull the working yarn through, ch1 to secure. Work R1 sts into the ring, pull the tail to close the ring once all sts have been made and secure by weaving the end in well.
	R	round	
	rep	repeat	
	sp/s	space/s	
	st/s	stitch/es	
	stch	starting chain	Used in place of the first st in a round. Is included in st count.
	stdg	standing	Attach yarn to your hook with a slip knot then work the st indicated as normal.
	yo	yarn over	Wrap yarn over hook from back to front.
Stitches UK/US			
.	ss	slip stitch	Insert hook into st or sp indicated, yo and pull through st or sp and loop on hook.
o	ch	chain	yo, pull through loop on hook.
+	dc / sc	double crochet / single crochet	Insert hook into st or sp indicated, yo, pull loop to front, yo, pull through both loops on hook.
T	htr / hdc	half treble crochet / half double crochet	Wrap yarn around hook, insert hook into st or sp indicated, yo, pull loop to front (3 loops on hook), yo, pull through all 3 loops on hook.
ꝉ	tr / dc	treble crochet / double crochet	Wrap yarn around hook, insert hook into st or sp indicated, yo, pull loop to front (3 loops on hook), 2x [yo, pull through 2 loops on hook].
ꝉ	dtr / tr	double treble crochet / triple crochet	Wrap yarn around hook twice, insert hook into st or sp indicated, yo, pull loop to front (4 loops on hook), 3x [yo, pull through 2 loops].
	crab st	crab stitch	Also known as reverse dc/sc. Work the dc/sc stitches in the opposite direction, working backwards around the blanket.

LEFT-HANDED CHARTS

1 Round Dot
Left-handed

2 Round Dot
Left-handed

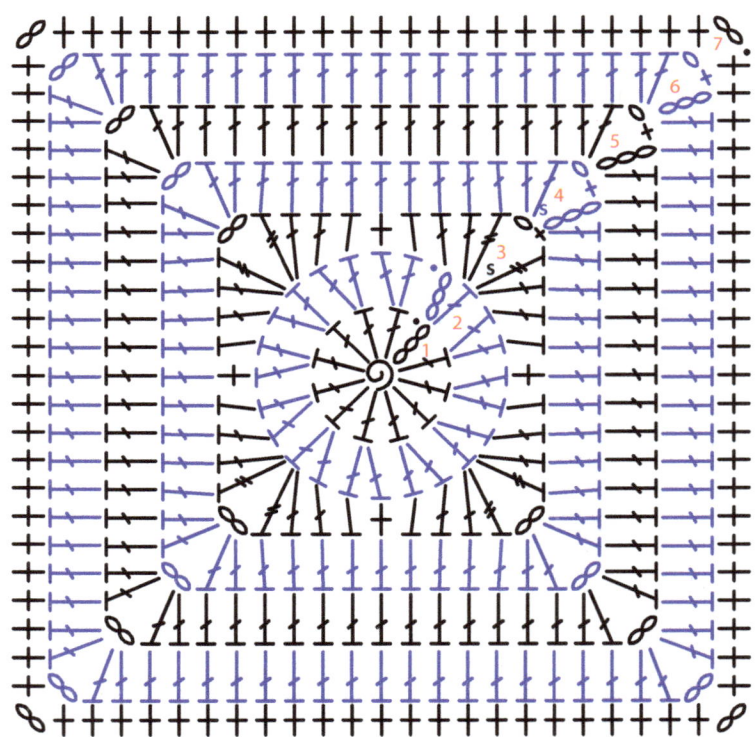

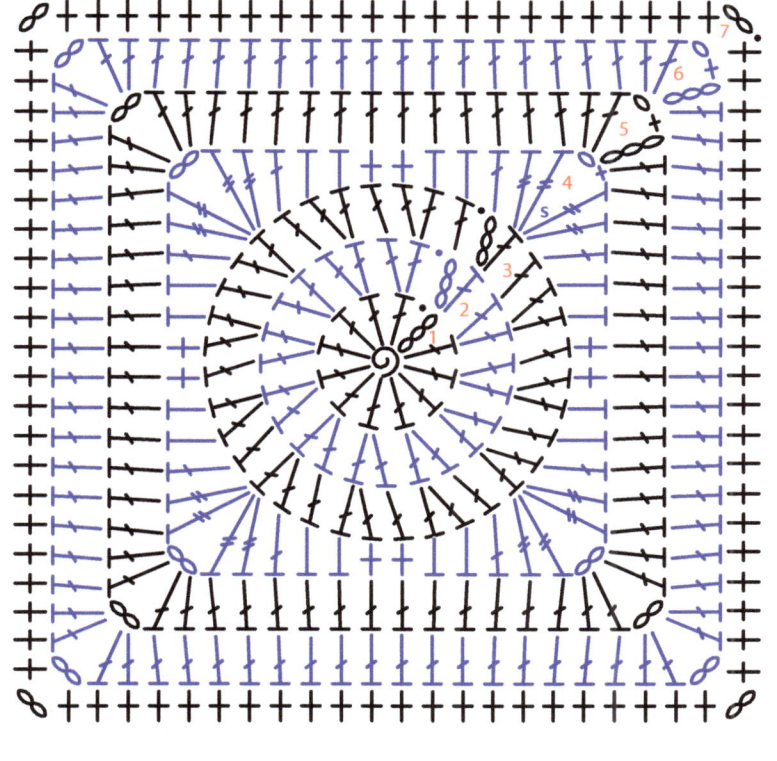

3 Round Dot Left-handed

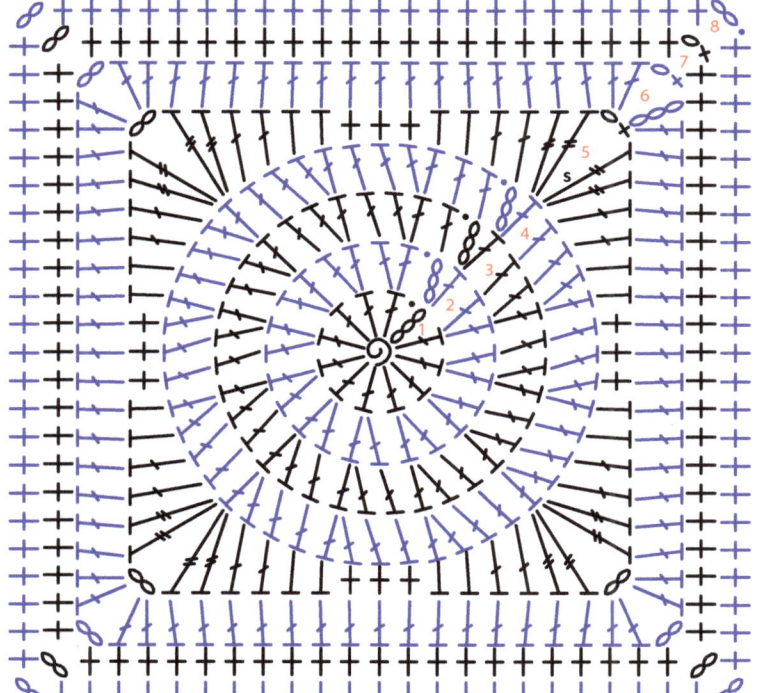

4 Round Dot Left-handed

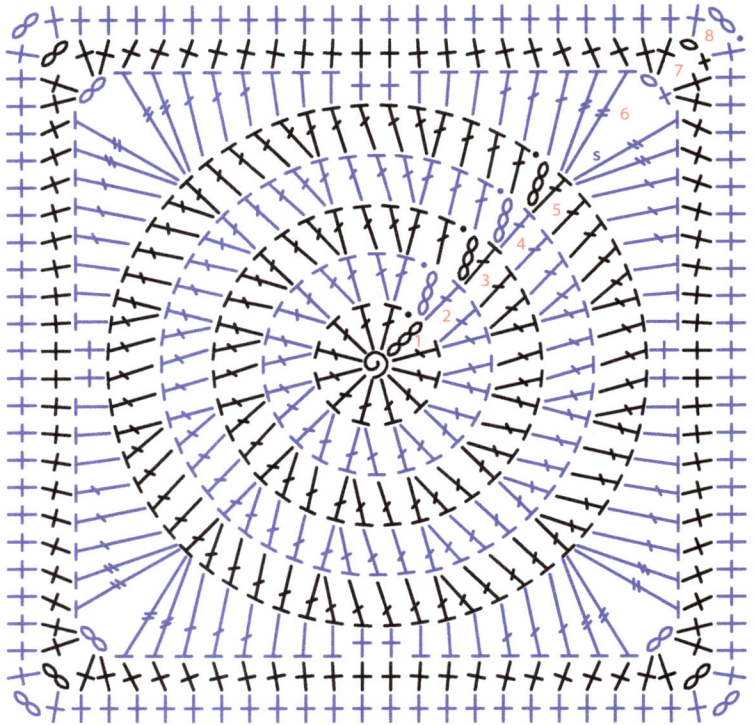

5 Round Dot Left-handed

HELPFUL LINKS

If you need a bit of extra help, head to
https://shelleyhusbandcrochet.com/dotty-spotty-helpful-links/ .
Enter the password DSHELP to access the page.

Here's what you'll find there:

- Video links for all the dot patterns
- Magic circle video
- Joining video
- False stitch information and video
- Invisible join information and video

Scan this QR code to download the free digital version of Dotty Spotty!

THANK YOU

My plan to revamp Dotty Spotty did not happen with me alone. I could not have done it without these awesome folks.

Thanks, Michelle Lorimer, for your graphic design prowess! You captured my fun style wishes so well.

Thank you, Jo O'Keefe, for the super cute blanket photography with newborn babe Vivienne and her Mum, Sally Coffey as the adorable models.

Thank you, SiewBee Pond, for your fab proofreading and tech-editing of all you see here.

Thanks to Amy Gunderson, for whipping up the charts in record time.

My pattern-testing team were wonderful as always. Thank you, Jenny Hebbard, Meghan McKenna, Ruth Bracey and Samantha Taylor for your super quick testing of the revamped patterns.

Thank you to Bendigo Woollen Mills for supplying the yarn for all the samples you see here.

And lastly, thank you for picking up my Dotty Spotty patterns to play with. I hope you create many much-loved gifts and family snuggles.

ABOUT THE AUTHOR

Shelley Husband is a prolific crochet pattern designer, publishing 6 books bursting with modern takes on the traditional granny square. Her first book, Granny Square Flair, won the best crochet book of 2019 in the UK.

Shelley has a real passion for designing seamless crochet patterns with the aim of teaching others through encouragingly supported patterns to create timeless, classic crochet heirlooms.

Based on Gunditjmara country also known as Narrawong in South West Victoria, Australia, when not designing and publishing new patterns, Shelley teaches crochet in person around Australia, and throughout the world via her online presence.

You can find Shelley online on most social media channels as spincushions.

MORE BOOKS

By Shelley Husband

Granny Square Academy

Learn all there is to know about making granny squares, including how to read patterns.

Beneath the Surface

A beginner friendly pattern, with lots of extra support including video links.

Granny Square Flair

50 written and charted granny square patterns and 11 project ideas to make with them.

Granny Square Patchwork

40 written and charted granny squares patterns of 6 sizes and 12 projects to make with them.

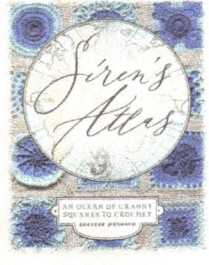

Siren's Atlas

64 written and charted granny square patterns for adventurous crocheters.

Nimue Crochet Blanket

A crochet quest of epic proportions with very detailed help including video links.

Buy my books direct from me in my shop or online at most online book retailers around the world.

Visit my pattern shop for digital patterns galore.

shop.shelleyhusbandcrochet.com